Wedding Accents & Accessories

Your wedding is a once-in-a-lifetime event. With a little creativity and some supplies found in most craft stores, you can have the wedding of your dreams without blowing your budget! Making your own headpiece can save a substantial amount of money. By adding a few satin flowers and pearls and attaching some tulle, a plain headband can become a beautiful veil, which could cost hundreds of dollars in a boutique. Best of all, you made it yourself!

The floral pieces for your wedding can also be made weeks ahead using silk flowers, again saving time and money. Corsages and boutonnieres, flower girl baskets and tosser bouquets can be created in a few evenings, using materials that are readily available. For a unique bridesmaid bouquet, consider the kissing ball on page 2—we've even included instructions for making a smaller version for your flower girl.

Changing the colors of the accessories to match your wedding is as simple as substituting flowers and ribbons in your colors. Saving money by making many of your own bridal accessories can ease the worry and help with the planning of your big day. It will be the wedding of your dreams!

Bridesmaid's Kissing Ball

one 5" wide pearl-studded ball with sheer white bow and hanger
$1^{1}/_{2}$" wide paper rose blossoms with 2" long leaves: 2 pink, 2 white
$^{1}/_{2}$" wide paper rosebuds with 1" long leaves: 4 pink, 4 white
seven $1^{1}/_{2}$"–3" wide ivy leaves
1 oz. of dried white baby's breath
low temperature glue gun and sticks

Glue six ivy leaves under the bow loops. Cut the rose blossom stems to $1^{1}/_{2}$" long and glue over the ivy leaves and under the loops. Glue the last ivy leaf among the rose blossoms. Cut 2 white and 2 pink rosebuds stems to 1" and the remaining rosebuds to 2" long. Glue the shorter stems angled up among the bow loops and the longer stems angled down among the ivy leaves. Cut the baby's breath to 1"–2" long and glue among the roses and leaves.

Flower Girl's Kissing Ball

one $3^{1}/_{2}$" wide pearl-studded ball with sheer white bow and hanger
six $1^{1}/_{2}$" wide ivy leaves
ten $^{1}/_{2}$" wide pink paper rosebuds with 1" long leaves
$^{1}/_{2}$ oz. of dried white baby's breath
low temperature glue gun and sticks

Glue the ivy leaves under the bow loops. Cut five rosebud stems to $^{1}/_{2}$" long and five to $1^{1}/_{2}$" long. Glue the short stems angled up among the bow loops and the longer bud stems angled down among the ivy. Cut the baby's breath to 1"–$1^{1}/_{2}$" long sprigs and glue among the flowers and ivy.

Christmas Kissing Ball

one $3^{1}/_{2}$" wide pearl-studded ball with sheer bow and hanger
40" length of $^{1}/_{4}$" wide red satin ribbon
five clusters of three $^{3}/_{4}$" wide white silk flowers with 1" long leaves and white berry clusters
one holly leaf pick with seven 2"–$2^{1}/_{2}$" long holly leaves with a 1" wide cluster of $^{1}/_{4}$" red berries
26-gauge wire
low temperature glue gun and sticks

Cut the holly leaves from the pick and glue under the bow loops as shown. Cut the ribbon in half and use each length to make a puffy bow (see inside the front cover) with a center loop and six $1^{1}/_{2}$" loops. Glue each bow on opposite sides of the hanger. Glue the flower clusters among the bow loops and cut the berry clusters in half. Glue them among the flowers and loops.

Flower Girl Basket

11"x8 1/2" white willow basket with a 8" tall handle
36"x54" ivory tulle
1 1/3 yards of 1 1/2" wide ivory ribbon
2 yards of 1/2" wide pearl and tulle trim
26-gauge wire
low temperature glue gun and sticks

1. Glue a 39" length of pearl/tulle trim around the outer edge of the basket. Starting at the base of one side of the handle, glue an end of the remaining pearl/tulle trim, then wrap it around the handle and glue at the base of the opposite handle.

2. Use the ribbon to make a puffy bow (see inside the front cover) with a center loop, six 2 1/2" loops and 6" tails. Trim the tails into an inverted "V". Glue the bow to the side of the basket below the handle. Use glue to tack the tails to the basket sides as shown. Fluff the tulle piece and place in the basket with the petals.

Designer Tip: *A large basket carried by a small girl in the wedding party is a darling sight for the guests. Consider filling it with silk petals, available by the box.*

Basket with Flower Rim

7 1/2"x4" round white willow basket with two 2" tall side handles
20" of 1/2" wide white pearl trim with tulle
one 4" wide bunch of 3/4" wide white silk flowers with white berry clusters and 1" long leaves
24" of 1/4" wide white sheer ribbon
24" of 1/4" wide white satin ribbon
low temperature glue gun and sticks

1. Glue the pearl/tulle trim around the top edge of the basket. Cut the flowers, berries and leaves from their stems. Glue them among the trim as shown.

2. Cut the ribbon lengths in half. Holding a sheer and white length together as one make a shoestring bow (see inside the front cover) with 1 1/2" loops and 3" tails. Repeat using the remaining ribbon. Glue a bow to each side of the basket under the handle.

Designer Tip: *This basket can be placed on the gift table to hold cards or used at a reception to hold favors to be passed out by attendants.*

Pink Wrist Corsage

1" wide white satin-covered elastic corsage band with metal clip
1 yard of $1/2$" wide metallic gold wire-edged sheer ribbon
1 yard of $3/8$" wide pink picot satin ribbon
five $5/8$" wide white silk rosebuds with 1" long leaves
one 4" wide cluster of $3/4$" wide pink silk flowers with 1" long leaves and berry clusters
26-gauge wire
low temperature glue gun and sticks

1 Use the gold ribbon to make a loopy bow (see inside the front cover) with eight 2" loops. Glue over the wire clip. Use the pink ribbon to make a loopy bow with a center loop, ten $1 1/2$" loops and 2" tails. Glue it to the center of the gold bow.

2 Cut the rosebuds from their stems and glue all of them around the pink bow's center loop. Cut the pink flower stems to $1 1/2$" long and glue them among the bow loops as shown.

Pink Boutonniere

6" of $1/2$" wide metallic gold wire-edged sheer ribbon
three $5/8$" wide white silk rosebuds with 1" long leaves
one cluster of three $3/4$" wide pink silk flowers with 1" long leaves and pink berry cluster
green floral tape
$1/8$" wide dowel or knitting needle
boutonniere pin
26-gauge wire

Form the ribbon into a 2" and a $2 1/2$" loop. Wire to secure. Cut the bud stems to 3", $2 1/2$" and 2" long and hold together as one as shown. Cut the pink flower cluster stem to $1 1/2$" and place to the left of the rose buds. Place the ribbon pick at the back. Wrap all of the stems with floral tape. Coil the end around the dowel to spiral. Insert a boutonniere pin at the back until ready to be worn.

Lavender Corsage

two 2" wide lavender paper rose blossoms with wire stems
five 1/2" wide white paper rosebuds with a 1" long leaf and wire stems
three 2" wide ivy leaves with 2" long stems
22" length of 1" wide white sheer ribbon
five 1"–2" wide sprigs of dried white baby's breath
green floral tape
pencil
26-gauge wire
corsage pin
low temperature glue gun and sticks

1 Hold the rose blossoms together and place two rosebuds to the left and three rosebuds to the upper right. Twist the stems together. Use the ribbon to make a puffy bow (see inside the front cover) with a center loop, six 1 1/4" long loops and 2" tails. Cut the tails into an inverted "V". Wire to secure, leaving 2" long wire tails. Place the bow wire below the 2 buds at the lower left.

2 Place the ivy leaves fanned out behind the buds and blossoms. Use floral tape to wrap all of the stems together. Wrap the stem around a pencil to coil. Glue baby's breath sprigs among the buds and blossoms. Place the pin in the stem until ready to be worn.

White Boutonniere

one 2" wide white paper rose blossom with wire stem
one 2" wide ivy leaf with 2" long stem
one 2" wide white baby's breath sprig
green floral tape
pencil
boutonniere pin
low temperature glue gun and sticks

Hold the rose stem with the ivy leaf behind it. Wrap both stems with the floral tape. Wrap the end around the pencil to coil. Glue the baby's breath between the leaf and the blossom. Place a pin in the stem until ready to be worn.

> Designer Tip: Mark each boutonniere and corsage with a tag noting to whom it should be given. Assign someone familiar with family members and special guests to ensure the appropriate people are given the flowers.

Wedding Veil

1" wide white satin covered headband
30"x40" white curly-edge corded two-layer veil
two 4" wide bunches of ³/₄" wide ivory silk flowers
two 4" wide bunches of ³/₄" wide white ribbon roses
wire cutters
low temperature glue gun and sticks

1 Use the wire cutters to clip the flowers from their stems. Beginning ¹/₂" from one end of the headband, glue white and ivory flowers on the center and sides of the satin band. Continue until the band is covered, stopping ¹/₂" from the end.

2 Gather the veil, if necessary, to 6" wide. (Some veils and pre-gathered and some have nylon line that must be pulled in order to gather the veil.) Center the veil inside the headband, gluing the gathered edge to the center back of the band, making sure the blusher veil is on top so that it may be pulled over the top of the headband and over the bride's face.

Tosser Bouquet

one 4" wide bouquet holder with foam base
one 7" wide ivory satin bouquet collar
one ivy bush with six 3"–7" sprigs of ³/₄"–1¹/₂" wide ivy leaves
4" wide clusters of ³/₄" wide silk flower blossoms: 2 pink, 3 white
1¹/₈ yards of ¹/₄" wide white satin ribbon
1¹/₈ yards of ¹/₄" wide pink satin ribbon
26-gauge wire
low temperature glue gun and sticks

1 Place the holder into the satin collar. Cut the ivy into fourteen 3"–4" long sprigs and glue to extend from the outer edge of the holder over the satin collar.

2 Cut the flower cluster stems to 3". Divide the pink into four clusters, and the white into six clusters. Glue a white cluster at the center of the holder. Glue the pink clusters evenly spaced around the white center cluster and then glue the remaining clusters around the pink.

3 Hold the ribbon lengths together as one. Make a loopy bow (see inside the front cover) with four 4" loops and 6"–8" staggered tails. Wire to secure and twist the wire ends to make a tail. Cut the wire tail to 2" and insert it at the bottom center of the bouquet among the ivy.

Hair Wreath

ivy garland with 1"–2" wide leaves
4 yards of 6" wide white tulle ribbon
thirteen 1 1/4" wide peach tulle flowers with 3/8" wide peach rose centers
one 4" wide cluster of 3/4" wide peach silk flowers with peach berry clusters and 1" long leaves
1 1/4 yards of 1/4" wide white sheer ribbon
1 1/4 yards of 1/4" wide white satin ribbon
green floral tape
measuring tape
low temperature glue gun and stick

1. Measure the wearer's head. Add 1 inch and cut the garland to this length. Using the floral tape, overlap and bind the ends to form a circle.

2. Cut the tulle ribbon in half and hold both lengths together as one in the center. At the center front of the wreath, begin winding one side with tulle ribbon around the garland and among the leaves. Repeat with the other side with both ends of the tulle ending at the back of the wreath. Tie the ends into a shoestring bow (see inside the front cover) with 2" loops and tails. Trim any excess tulle. Puff the tulle in the ivy leaves by pulling it apart slightly.

3. Hold the satin ribbon lengths together and tie into a shoestring bow with 2" loops and 18" tails. Glue the ribbon bow to the center of the tulle bow. Glue a tulle flower to the center of the bows.

4. Cut the peach silk flowers into groups of three flowers with a berry cluster, two leaves and 1" long stems. Cut the remaining tulle flowers from their stems and glue the flowers and clusters among the tulle and leaves.

Hair Bow

25" length of 1 1/2" wide lavender satin ribbon
24" lengths of 1/4" wide satin ribbon: 1 white, 1 pink, 1 lavender
3" long hair clip
four 3/4" wide clay rose blossoms: 2 pink, 1 ivory, 1 lavender
26-gauge white cloth covered wire
low temperature glue gun and sticks

Use the 1 1/2" wide ribbon to make a loopy bow (see inside the front cover) with four 3" loops. Glue the bow to the top of the hair clip. Hold the three 1/4" ribbons together as one. Make a loopy bow with four 1 1/2" long loops. Wire to secure, trim the wire and glue to the center of the lavender bow. Glue the clay flowers to the bow center in a cluster as shown.

Decorations & Accents

The warm glow from candles bring romance to a wedding ceremony, as well as the reception, and become important accents. We've designed a variety of decorated candles that can be included in your wedding. Glass bowls holding tapers and decorated with silk flowers, luminaries in candle rings, a unity candle with decorated lighting tapers and several votive cups are all featured here.

The candle rings used in these projects are purchased items which have been dressed up with additional materials, taking them beyond the standard fare for floral decorations. Whether the votive cups are placed around the reception area or among flowers at the wedding, they provide the perfect ambiance.

Decorating the cake knife and server adds a romantic touch to a reception while the handcrafted cake top provides the finishing touch. The same decorations used on the serving pieces can also be duplicated to use on the toasting glasses, making it easy to plan all the decorations.

While all the materials used in these designs can be found in most craft stores, your creativity in putting them together brings your personal touch to your wedding, making it unique and special.

Ivy Bowl with Candle

battery-operated lighted white floral wreath with 4³/8" wide base and 2¹/4" wide white organza flowers with pearl stamens
5¹/4"x5¹/4" clear glass ivy bowl
8" wide floral candle ring with four 2" wide yellow dogwoods, one 4" wide lily, four 1"–3" wide ivory to dark yellow rosebuds and blossoms, many 2"–4" wide ivy leaves and 1¹/2"–3" long rose leaves
2 yards of ³/4" wide metallic gold sheer ribbon
one cup of 8-10mm clear glass flat backed marbles
one green plastic candle spike for a taper candle
12" tall white taper candle
E-6000 glue
two "C" batteries
24-gauge wire
wire cutters

1. Use the wire cutters to cut the spike from the bottom of the plastic candle holder. Glue the base of the holder into the bottom center of the ivy bowl. Let dry overnight.

2. Use the ribbon to make a puffy bow (see inside the front cover) with a center loop, twelve 2" loops and one 12" long tail. Glue the tail end to the bowl neck and wrap the ribbon around the neck, gluing the bow over the tail end. Place the candle in the holder and then add the marbles to cover the holder base.

3. Place the floral candle ring over the lighted ring and gently pull the white flowers through the silk flowers. Place the ivy bowl inside the candle rings. Insert the batteries and hide the battery holder among the flowers.

Ivy Bowl Wrapped in Tulle

5¹/4"x5¹/4" clear glass ivy bowl
two 18" squares of ivory tulle
20" length of 1¹/2" wide ivory satin ribbon
2"x2" clear glass votive holder
ivory votive candle
24-gauge white fabric covered wire

Layer the squares and place the ivy bowl in the center. Gather the edges up around the neck of the bowl and secure with the wire. Wrap the ribbon around the neck and tie in an overhand knot (see inside the front cover). Trim the tails to 2" long with an inverted "V". Place the candle in the holder and the holder into the bowl.

Designer Tip: These centerpieces are very easy to assemble. Consider giving them as thank you gifts to special helpers or relatives.

Topiary with Lavender Accents

17" tall white rose double-ball topiary with a white urn and white sheer bow
two 18" squares of lavender tulle
34" of 1½" wide lavender satin ribbon
one 4" wide cluster of ¾" wide lavender silk flowers, berry clusters and 1" long leaves
two 12" lengths of ¼" wide lavender satin ribbon
low temperature glue gun and sticks

1 Glue a cluster of 3 flowers and leaves at the top of the small flower ball. Glue 5 clusters of 3 flowers with berries and leaves around the top of the large flower ball. Glue 9 individual flower blossoms around the base of the topiary trunk.

2 Hold the ¼" wide ribbons together as one. Tie a shoestring bow (see inside the front cover) with 1½" loops and 3" tails around the trunk of the topiary between the flower balls as shown.

3 Remove the sheer bow from the urn and discard. Layer the tulle and gather up around the urn sides. Wrap the 1½" ribbon around the center of the urn sides and tie in a shoestring bow with 2" loops and 3" tails. Cut the tails into an inverted "V".

Designer Tip: These topiaries can be used in a variety of charming ways such as alternating them with luminaries along a walk or driveway, placing them at the end of a pews or lining alter steps.

Topiary with Pink Accents

17" tall white rose-covered cone in a white urn with bow and pearl accents
one 4" wide bunch of ¾" wide mauve silk flowers with yellow centers, clusters of ½" wide berries and 1" long leaves
1 yard of 6" wide mauve tulle ribbon
two 4" lengths of 26-gauge wire
low temperature glue gun and sticks

1. Wrap a wire length around one end of the tulle ribbon and insert into the moss at the base of the topiary trunk. Twist the tulle until it measures 1½" wide, then wrap it in a spiral fashion between the pearl garland as shown. Wrap wire around the tulle end and insert it into the top of the topiary among the roses.

2. Cut the flower stems to 2" long. Set one blossom aside and glue the rest in the urn around the base of the topiary. Glue the remaining blossom to the bow center.

Designer Tip: *These pre-made topiaries are easy to embellish with a color scheme matching your wedding. They can be placed at the center of each guest table or in pairs on a buffet table.*

Luminary in Candle Ring

4"x5" iridescent white ceramic luminary with bell cut-outs
8" wide floral candle ring with 4" wide cluster of peach hydrangea blossoms, five 1¾" wide purple hydrangea blossoms, 4½" wide peach lily, 1"–3" wide peach and pink rosebuds and blossoms, 2"–3" wide ivy leaves and 1½"–3" long rose leaves
tea light candle

Place the luminary into the center of the candle ring. Place the tea light in the luminary. Light the candle just before the guests arrive.

> *Designer Tip:* These luminaries provide a wonderful romantic glow when used at evening weddings. Use them to line a garden path or driveway for an evening wedding.
>
> For an "at home" wedding, place the luminaries ascending a staircase. Place them on every other stair, being careful not to block the path of the guests.

Lighted Arch with Tulle

8' white lighted wedding arch
14 yards of 54" wide white tulle
6' of grape leaf garland with 2"–4" wide leaves
26-gauge white cloth covered wire
wire cutters

Designer Tip: *Chose one of the many lighting options available with the arch and place it at the entrance to your garden wedding or at the alter.*

1. Assemble the arch according to the manufacturer's directions.

2. Cut the tulle into a 6-yard and 8-yard length. Drape the 6-yard length over the top and sides of the arch. Let the ends fall to the ground in graceful billows. Use wire to secure the center of the 8 yard length to the top center of the arch. Measure 20" to the right and wire the tulle to the arch curve. Measure 20" from this point and wire again. Fluff the areas between the wires. Repeat for the opposite side of the arch.

3. Gather the bottom edge of the tulle at each side of the arch and wire it to the bottom front of the arch. Allow the excess yardage to billow over the secured bottom edge as if it were a balloon.

4. Cut the garland into four 18" lengths. Wire two vertically to the left and right sides as shown. Wire a length under the arch top and the last length horizontally at the arch top.

Unity Candle with Lighting Tapers

4¹/₂" wide clear acrylic cake top base
two 2¹/₂" tall glass candle holders
forty-four ³/₄" wide clay roses with 1" long leaves in assorted pastel colors
candles: 9"x3" white pillar and two 1¹/₂"x10" white tapers
²/₃ yard of 1¹/₂" wide white satin ribbon
2²/₃ yards of ¹/₈" wide white satin ribbon
wire cutters
liquid acrylic sealer
¹/₂" wide flat paintbrush
low temperature glue gun and sticks

1 Apply sealer around the top rim of the acrylic base. Let dry. Use the wire cutters to clip the rose blossoms and leaves from the stems. Set aside a yellow and pink rose and four leaves for step 3. Glue two rows of roses around the top edge of the cake top base, positioning them in different directions. Glue the leaves among the roses.

2 Tie the 1¹/₂" wide ribbon around the center of the pillar candle in a shoestring bow with 2" loops and 3" tails. Cut the tails into an inverted "V". Place the pillar on the base.

3 Cut the ¹/₈" wide ribbon into four equal lengths. Hold two lengths together and tie them around the center of the glass candle holder in a shoestring bow (see inside the front cover) with 1¹/₂" loops and tails. Repeat for the other holder. Glue a yellow rose with two leaves at the center of one bow and a pink rose with two leaves on the second holder.

Square Votive

2 1/2"x2 3/4" ivory candle in clear glass holder
18" length of 1/8" wide satin ribbons: white, ivory
two ivory and one white 3/4" wide silk flowers
two gold metal "wedding rings"
low temperature glue gun and sticks

Hold the ribbon lengths together as one. Wrap them around the top edge of the holder and tie into a shoestring bow (see inside the front cover) with 1" loops and 1 1/2" tails. Glue the flowers to the center of the bow. Glue the rings to extend from under the flowers.

Ivory Votive

2"x1 1/4" clear glass votive cup
12" of 1/4" wide ivory satin ribbon
one 3/4" wide white silk flower
ivory votive candle
low temperature glue gun and sticks

Wrap the ribbon around the center of the votive cup and tie into a shoestring bow (see inside the front cover). Glue the back of the ribbon to the cup to keep it from slipping. Glue the flower to the bow center. Place the candle in the cup.

Pearl-Studded Votive Cup

2 1/2"x2 3/4" green glass votive holder
15" of 1/4" wide white satin ribbon
ivory flat-backed pearls: one 10mm, eight 8mm
white votive candle
low temperature glue gun and sticks

Wrap the ribbon around the top edge of the holder and tie into a shoestring bow (see inside the front cover). Glue the back of the ribbon to the votive cup to keep it from slipping. Glue the 10mm pearl to the bow center. Glue the 8mm pearls staggered around the side of the votive cup as shown. Place the candle in the holder.

Ivy Bowl with Pearl Accents

5¼"x5¼" clear glass ivy bowl
2¼"x2½" pearl studded votive holder with candle
1 yard of 3mm white fused pearls
tacky craft glue

Turn the bowl upside down and run a line of glue around the base. Press a 10" length of pearls into the glue and let dry. Turn the bowl over and glue the votive holder into the bottom of the bowl to secure. Wrap the remaining pearls around the bowl neck twice and knot to secure. Knot the tail ends. Place a dot of glue on the knots and let dry.

Ivory Pillar in Cylinder

3½"x7½" clear glass vase
2¾"x6½" tall ivory pillar candle
22" of 2½" wide sheer ivory wire edged ribbon
one 3" cluster of ¾" wide white silk flowers with 1" long leaves and 4" long wire stems
four 1½"–2½" wide variegated ivy leaves
green floral tape
pencil
low temperature glue gun and sticks

1 Place the candle inside the vase. Wrap the ribbon around the vase 2" from the bottom edge. Knot the ribbon and trim the tails to 4" long. Cut the tails into an inverted "V".

2 Wrap the flower cluster with floral tape and wind around the pencil to coil. Tuck the flower stem behind the knot and glue. Glue the ivy leaves around the knot as shown.

Candle in Terra Cotta Pot

6"x5 3/4" terra cotta pot
2 3/4"x7 1/2" white pillar candle
24" of 3/8" wide picot ribbon: pink, white and lavender
4" wide clusters of 3/4" wide silk flowers with 1" long leaves and berry clusters: pink, blue and lavender
4" wide cluster of 3/4" wide white daisies with yellow centers
8"x4"x3" block of floral foam for dried and silk flowers
liquid acrylic sealer
white acrylic paint
1" wide foam brush
serrated knife
low temperature glue gun and sticks

1. Apply the sealer to the pot and let dry. Apply three coats of white paint, letting each coat dry between applications. Seal again and let dry.

2. Cut the foam to 6" long and glue into the center of the pot. Cut the remaining foam into 4 equal pieces and glue around the foam in the pot to fill the holes. Place the candle on the center of the foam.

3. Cut the flowers into 1 1/2" long stems and, alternating colors, glue around the candle, covering the foam and extending over the edge of the pot.

4. Hold the ribbons as one and wrap around the center of the candle. Tie a shoestring bow (see inside the front cover) with 1 1/2" loops and staggered 3"–4" tails.

3

Ivy Bowl Votive Holder

4"x4" clear glass ball bowl
16" of 1 1/2" wide ivory satin ribbon
three 1 1/2" wide variegated silk ivy leaves
three 3/4" wide ivory clay rose blossoms
eight 2"-2 1/2" long dried plumosus sprigs
ivory votive candle
low temperature glue gun and sticks

Fold the ribbon in half width-wise and wrap around the neck of the bowl. Tie in an overhand knot (see inside the front cover) and trim the tails to 3" long. Cut the tails into an inverted "V". Glue the ivy leaves to the knot. Glue the rose blossoms at the center of the leaves with the plumosus glued evenly spaced among the roses. Place the candle in the ball.

Decorated Cake Knife & Server

2 yards of 3/8" wide white picot satin ribbon
four 3/4" wide gold plastic wedding rings, each with a
    1" wide white plastic dove
26-gauge white cloth covered wire
cake knife and server
low temperature glue gun and sticks

Use a 24" length of ribbon to make a loopy bow (see inside the front cover) with six 1 1/2" long loops. Cut two 6"–7" lengths of ribbon and place at the back of the bow and secure with the wire. Place one dove inside the other ring and glue both to the center of the bow. Secure the bow to the knife set by tying one set of tails around the knife and the server handles.

Toasting Glass Embellishments

six 3/4" wide foam rose blossoms with 1" long leaves:
    two mauve, two pink, two ivory
48" of 1/4" wide pink satin ribbon
green floral tape
1/8" wide dowel or knitting needle
set of toasting glasses

Hold one rose of each color together. Cut the stems to 3" long and tape with floral tape. Wrap the taped stem around the dowel to spiral. Cut the ribbon into four 12" lengths. Use one length to make a loopy bow (see inside the front cover) with four 1 1/2" loops. Secure the center of the bow with a 12" length of ribbon. Place the bow at the top of the spiraled stem and knot the ribbon at the back of the stem. Repeat for a second set of flowers and bow. Secure the bow to the glasses by tying the bow tails around the base of the glass.

Designer Tip: *A dot of tacky craft glue will help hold the bows in place and will be water soluble.*

Swan Cake Topper

4½" white plastic cake top base with hearts
1½" tall ivory plastic swan
30" of ⅛" wide lavender satin ribbon
½" wide paper rosebuds with 1" long leaves and wire
  stems: 16 white, 5 lavender
1 oz. of dried plumosus sprigs
2" wide foam ball
serrated knife
26-gauge wire
low temperature glue gun and sticks

1 Use the knife to cut the foam ball in half. Glue one-half to the center of the cake top base. Glue the swan in front of the foam base.

2 Cut one 5", five 4", eight 2½" and two 1½" long white roses. Cut one 4½", two 3½", two 1½" long lavender roses. Place the 5" white in the center of the foam with the 4½" lavender in front, bent forward. Glue the 4" white roses evenly spaced around center roses, facing front and back. Glue the 3½" lavender roses on both ends of the swan. Insert the 2½" white roses evenly spaced around the front and back of the base. Glue the 1½" long roses extending from the bottom of the foam, lavender at the front and white at the back.

3 Cut the plumosus into 2"–7" sprigs and insert into the foam evenly spaced as shown in the large photo. Use the ribbon to make a loopy bow (see inside the front cover) with six 2" loops and 3" tails. Wire to secure, leaving 1" long wire tails. Twist the tails together and insert into the foam to the right of the swan.

Designer Tip: *Make a cake decoration for each tier. Place them on the center of each tier. Remove them before cutting the cake.*

Cake Tier Decoration

2" wide paper roses with wire stems: 2 white,
  1 lavender
1 1/6 yards of ⅛" wide lavender satin ribbon
six 2"–3" long plumosus sprigs
26-gauge wire
low temperature glue gun and sticks

Cluster the roses together and twist the wire stems together at the base. Cut the stems to ½" long. Place glue between the roses to secure. Use the ribbon to make a loopy bow (see inside the front cover) with eight 2½" loops. Glue the bow under the roses. Glue the plumosus between the blossoms.

Ribbons & Bows

You'll find bows to be one of the easiest and most versatile decorations for your wedding and reception—all the while being one of the prettiest accents, too! Large white bows made with wired ribbon are beautiful and dramatic, bringing an elegant feeling to the ceremony. And one of the easiest pew decorations is a large bow made from tulle or ribbon with a few silk flowers glued among the loops. So easy, yet so pretty!

Tulle, whether in colors or white, is simple to us, yet adds a dramatic effect to the wedding or reception. Often, a simple draping of tulle around the cake or a floral decoration can soften the look and add a romance to the entire room. Draping tulle from pew to pew adds a softness and sometimes whimsical feeling to the aisle in a church while an outdoor wedding can become an enchanted fairyland when the processional path is bordered with tulle garlands.

Combining ribbon bows over large, fluffy tulle bows provides a finishing touch to decorations both in the wedding and the reception while adding drama with very little cost. Attach the bows to a large candelabra to create a striking embellishment. Or use a large bow to secure tulle bunting in loops around the edge of a serving table. Tulle and ribbon bows to add charm and grace to a wedding or reception very easily—and whether making them yourself or using premade bows, you're able to save money while creating the wedding of your dreams!

Stairway Decorations

white tulle garland with 3mm white iridescent fused pearls and 1/4" wide white gimp braid as needed to cover stair banister
7" wide white acetate pre-made bow
ivy bush with many 4"–15" long stems of 1"–2" wide leaves
1 1/4 yards of white 3mm fused pearls
white painters tape (tape that will not damage surfaces)
26-gauge white cloth-covered wire
low temperature glue gun and sticks

1 Remove the tulle garland from the spool and use the tape to secure the end to the bottom of the newel post. Begin wrapping up the post and around and over the banister, spacing evenly between posts. *To join more than one length of garland:* Join the garlands end to end, using the white wire to secure. Continue wrapping the banister until you reach the top.

2 After wrapping the banister, fluff the garland by separating the tulle layers and bringing the pearls and braid around to the top of the garland.

3 *Bow:* Cut the ivy stems from the main stem. Glue four 4" lengths among the bow loops. Glue a 15", and two 9" lengths to trail from under the bow and lay among the tails. Cut the pearls into a 24" and an 18" length. Form each into a loop by holding the ends together and gluing the ends under the bow loops so that the pearls hang down among the ivy. Wire the bow to the newel post as shown.

Cake Table Decorations

white 54" wide tulle to fit around the perimeter of the table
5" wide white acetate pre-made bows
white floor length round tablecloth
pink and yellow silk rose petals
corsage pins

1 To determine how much tulle will be needed for each table, measure the circumference of the table and double the amount. Place the cloth on the table. Place something heavy at the center of the table so the cloth does not slide off as you work. Begin at what will be the back of the cake table. Gather one end of the tulle in your hand and place the tulle behind a bow, wrapping the bow's chenille stem around the tulle and twisting to secure. Use a corsage pin to secure the bow and tulle to the edge of the tablecloth with the pins pointing down. Gather 36" of tulle into a tube shape and secure with another bow. Run the gathered tulle loosely around the edge of the table as shown. Continue until the table is edged with the tulle. Cut the tulle and remove the first bow from the cloth and wire the ends together behind the bow. Replace the bow.

2 Pull the underside of the tulle downward to create a "scalloped" shape. Repeat making "scallops" until the back of the table is reached.

3 *Petals:* Gently place silk rose petals among the tulle layers. Sprinkle some petals on the table top.

Candelabra with Garland

8" wide sheer white pre-made bow
*24" of ivy garland with many 1"–4" wide leaves,
 many 2"–5" wide white lily blossoms and buds and
 1"–2 1/2" wide white rose blossoms and buds*
gold candelabra
seven white taper candles
26-gauge wire

Wire the garland to the front of the candelabra and secure the bow at the center. Place the candles in the holders.

Pew Bow with Flowers

8" wide white sheer pre-made bow
*24" of ivy garland with many 1"–4" wide leaves,
 many 2"–5" wide white lily blossoms and buds and
 1"–2 1/2" wide white rose blossoms and buds*
pew bow clip or white painters tape

1. Form the garland into a tear drop shape by holding the ends together. Secure the ends behind the bow with the bow's chenille stem. The flowers will hang down under the bow with the bow tails among the greenery.

2. Attach the chenille stem to the bow clip or tape the stem to the pew with painters tape.

> **Designer Tip:** You can make 3 pew decorations with a 6' floral garland. Choose a garland that is full and lush looking.

Tulle Aisle Garland with Bows

7" wide white acetate pre-made bows
bolts of 54" wide white tulle
white painter's tape or pew bow clips

1 Secure each end of the tulle behind a bow using the bow's chenille stem. Secure a bow to the first and last pew on the aisle with a pew clip or use painter's tape that will not harm the finish.

2 At the center pew, secure the tulle to the bow and the bow to the pew so there are 2 equal "scallops". Using the bows, make smaller scallops between each pew and secure with a pew clip or painter's tape. Adjust as needed so they are all equal. Tulle looks best when it's full and bountiful. Place or glue individual silk ivy leaves and rose petals among the layers of tulle for a lovely and graceful look.

Measuring: To determine how much tulle you'll need, measure the distance from the first pew to the last and double this length. This will be enough for one side of the aisle.

Designer Tip: Consult with the church's staff to see what is preferred for use when hanging tulle and pew bows. Do this before purchasing your decorations.

Garden Path Aisle

4' long wood garden stakes
7" wide white pre-made acetate bows
54" wide white tulle
white latex paint
mini foam paint roller
hammer or rubber mallet
tape measure

1. You will need 1 stake for every 4'–5' of the "aisle". For example: if your aisle is 30' long you would need 7 stakes x 2 (for both sides of the aisle) = 14. Use the foam roller to paint the stakes. Let dry.

2. Use the hammer or rubber mallet to place the stakes in the ground. Using the chenille stem wire on the bow, attach the bow to the tulle center. Follow the directions for making the "tulle aisle garland" (see page 23) to evenly hang the tulle from each stake.

Designer Tip: To determine how much tulle you'll need measure between two stakes, allowing the tape measure to drape into the scallop depth you desire. Multiply this measurement by the number of spaces between the stakes. Add to this the length of tulle that will fall from each end stake.

Reception Buffet Table

one strand of white bow lights
white floor length tablecloth
4 yards of 54" wide white tulle
5" wide lavender wired tulle ribbon
corsage pins
26-gauge white cloth-covered wire
wire cutters
white extension cord
6' long buffet table

Use the ribbon to make three puffy bows (see inside the front cover) with a center loop, six 3" loops and two 6" long tails, securing with cloth-covered wire. Place the cloth on the table. Find the center of the white tulle and the lighted bow strand, then beginning at the center of the table, wire the tulle and strand to the back of one bow. Twist the wire to secure. Use a corsage pin to attach the bow back to the edge of the tablecloth. Allow for slack in the tulle and lights to form "scallops" and repeat at each end of the table.

Buffet Basket

14" wide natural basket with 8" ball handle
1 yard of 54" wide lavender tulle
1 1/2 yards of 1 1/2" wide lavender satin ribbon
1 1/2 yards of 5" wide lavender wired tulle ribbon
26-gauge white cloth-covered wire
wire cutters
low temperature glue gun and sticks

Glue one end of the satin ribbon to the base of the basket handle. Wrap around the handle, overlapping the ribbon, and glue to the base of the other handle. Use the wire tulle to make a puffy bow (see inside the front cover) with a 4" center loop and six 4" long loops. Wire it to the base of the handle. Place the tulle in the basket.

At the reception: Fill with bread or rolls and place on the buffet table.

Page 25

Invitations & Gift Wrap

Making your own wedding invitations, programs, place cards and thank-you notes may seem overwhelming, but here you'll see how simple it can be to create all your printed needs and coordinate them for a perfect look. And best of all, you'll save money and time! Whether you frame the place cards or print them on folded card stock and embellish them with a bow or ribbon rose, those small touches add elegance to the reception.

Wrap all those special gifts and mementos for those who share your moment in elegant and pretty wrappings. Plain paper decorated with stamped images, then covered in tulle and embellished with flowers and bows become dramatic gifts. The charming remembrances for your attendants and helpers will be treasured for years because they have your personal touch.

Bath Accessories Wrapped in Organza Bag

5"x7" ivory organza drawstring bag
three ¾" wide ivory clay roses each with one 1" long leaves
bath accessories: beads, soap and salts
low temperature glue gun and sticks

Place the bath accessories in the bag and draw the string. Tie in a shoestring bow (see inside the front cover). Cut the roses and leaves from their stems. Glue the roses and leaves to the bow with the leaves behind the roses as shown.

> **Designer Tip:** *This bag full of personal luxury makes the perfect attendant's gift. Add a gift certificate for a manicure in the bag for the perfect pampering touch.*

Stamped Gift Box

8"x4" round papier mâché box
1½" yards of 5½" white wire-edged tulle ribbon
acrylic paints: white, pink
1¾" long bouquet foam stamp
1" wide flat paintbrush
liquid acrylic sealer
paper plate
paper towel
26-gauge white wire
low temperature glue gun and sticks

1. Seal the box and the lid. Let dry. Paint the box white and the lid pink. Let dry.

2. Pour a small amount of pink paint onto the paper plate. Dip the stamp into the paint and blot the excess on the paper towel. Begin stamping the image around the box, turning the stamp at different angles as you stamp. Let dry. Apply sealer to both the box and lid and let dry.

3. Use the ribbon to make a puffy bow (see inside the front cover) with a center loop, six 4" loops and 6" tails. Glue the center of the bow to the lid. Extend the tails to opposite sides of the lid and glue the ends to the underside.

Wedding Invitation

Paper Flair™ 5"x6 1/2" blank white card and envelope
Paper Pizazz™ specialty silver paper
9" of 1/4" wide white satin ribbon
metallic silver acrylic paint
2" wide double heart foam stamp
solid white paper
computer and printer
newspaper, paper plate
glue stick

1. Cut the card in half at the fold. Place the card on the newspaper. Pour a small amount of paint on the paper plate and dip the stamp. Blot the stamp on the newspaper to remove the excess paint, then stamp randomly on the card front at different angles and off the card edge. Let dry.

2. Print your text on white paper. Trim it to 3"x4 1/4" and mat on silver paper leaving a 1/8" border. Glue it to the center of the stamped card. Using the ribbon, make a shoestring bow (see inside the front cover) with 1" loops and 1 1/2" tails. Glue it centered on the silver mat above the text.

3. *Envelope*: Open the envelope and place face down on the newspaper. Cover the body of the envelope so only the flap is exposed. Stamp as for the card and let dry.

Wedding Program

Paper Pizazz™ dark green suede paper
solid dark ivory paper
1 3/4" wide double-ring foam stamp
gold acrylic paint
paper plate
paper towel
computer and printer
glue stick

1. Print the text vertically on the ivory paper leaving a 1 1/2" margin at the top. Cut the paper to 3 3/4"x10".

2. Pour a small amount of paint on the paper plate and dip the stamp. Blot the excess paint on the paper towel. Stamp above the printed text. Let dry. Glue the program centered on a 4 1/8"x11" strip of green suede paper.

Thank You Card

Paper Flair™ 5"x6 1/2" ivory blank card and envelope
Paper Pizazz™ 12"x12" white roses patterned paper
Paper Pizazz™ specialty gold paper
solid ivory paper
2" wide wedding bells foam stamp
gold acrylic paint
old toothbrush
newspaper, paper plate
glue stick
computer and printer

1. Open the card and cut a 1 3/4" wide strip from the long right edge of the card front. Cover the remaining card front with the white roses paper. Using the computer, write "Thank You" and print on ivory paper. Cut the paper to a 4 1/4"x1 1/2" rectangle and mat it on the gold paper, leaving a 1/8" border. Glue it centered on the roses paper.

2. Place the card on the newspaper. Pour the paint on a paper plate. Dip the moistened toothbrush into the gold paint. Lightly spatter the card with gold paint and let dry. Dip the foam stamp into gold paint and blot off the excess on the newspaper. Stamp three bells on the bottom ivory border of the card. Let dry.

Card with Bow & Flower

3"x4" ivory card
9" of ¼" wide white satin ribbon
⅝" wide white ribbon rose
fine point black pen
low temperature glue gun and sticks

Write the name on the card and fold it in half to 3"x2". Use the ribbon to make a shoestring bow (see inside the front cover) and glue it centered at the top of the card. Glue the rose to the bow center.

Bow with Blue Flower Card

3"x 4" white pre-lined place card
7" of ¼" wide white satin ribbon
fine point blue pen
one ¾" wide blue silk flower with 1" long leaf
low tempature glue gun and sticks

Write the name on the card. Use the ribbon to tie a shoestring bow (see inside the front cover) and glue it to the upper left corner. Glue the flower and leaf to the bow center.

Spattered Card

3"x4" white card
9" of ¼" wide lavender satin ribbon
Paper Pizazz™ lavender satin patterned paper
solid white paper
computer and printer
lavender acrylic paint
old toothbrush, newspaper
low temperature glue gun and sticks

Place the cards on the newspaper. Dip the moistened toothbrush in the paint and spatter (see inside the front cover) a light mist of paint onto the cards. Let dry. Print the guest's name and table number. Cut the paper to 2"x¾" and mat on lavender satin paper, leaving a ⅛" border. Glue it centered on the folded place card. Use the ribbon to tie a shoestring bow and glue it to the upper left corner.

Computer Lettered Card

3"x4" white card with silver edge
7" of ⅛" wide white satin ribbon
white and black paper
computer and printer
low temperature glue gun and sticks

Using your home computer and printer can quickly produce uniform results. Cut the typed names into 1⅞"x¾" wide strips. Mat on black, leaving ⅛" border, and glue each centered on ae card. Use the ribbon to make shoestring bow (see inside the front cover) and glue it centered above the name.

Card with Chalked Accents

3"x4" white card with embossed bells and roses
fine point metallic gold pen
dark pink and green decorative chalk
#0 liner paintbrush

Chalking adds a hint of color to these pre-embossed cards. Using a dry paintbrush, lightly run the bristles over the chalk and then touch the areas to be chalked. Wash and dry the brush when changing colors. Write the name on the card.

Double Wedding Ring Card

3"x4" white card with ivory border
two gold metal wedding rings
9" of ¼" wide sheer white ribbon
fine tip black pen
low temperature glue gun and sticks

Write the name in black on the card. Thread the rings onto the ribbon and tie a shoestring bow (see inside the front cover). Glue it centered at the top of the folded card.

Organza Photo Frame

3"x4" ivory organza frame with a 2"x3" oval opening
six ¾" wide ivory clay roses with a 1" long leaf
wire cutters
photograph
low temperature glue gun and sticks

Use the wire cutters to cut the roses from the stems. Glue a cluster of 3 roses to the top left and bottom right of the vertical frame. Cut the leaves from the stems and glue them as shown. Place the photo in the frame.

Designer Tip: *Have individual photos taken with your attendants and special helpers. Frame and present them as a thank-you remembrance of this special day.*

Organza Place Card Frame

3"x4" white organza frame with a 2"x3" oval opening
¾" wide silk flowers: 7 white, 7 pink
9" of ⅞" wide pink organza ribbon
Paper Pizazz™ pink moiré patterned paper
computer and printer
low temperature glue gun and sticks

1. Place the frame horizontally. Use the ribbon to make a shoestring bow (see inside the front cover). Glue it to the frame as shown. Glue a white flower to the bow center. Alternate gluing pink and white flowers around the oval opening.

2. Use the computer and printer to type the guest name and table number. Print it onto patterned paper and cut to fit in the frame.

Designer Tip: *It's nice to add information about the relationship of the guest to the bride and groom. It offers a conversation opener for the other guests at the table.*

Silver Rose Photo Frame

4"x3 1/4" silver frame with embossed roses photograph

Choosing a photo from your courtship or your engagement makes a charming gift for family and friends.

Silver Frame Thank You

4"x3 1/4" silver frame
9" of 3/8" wide white satin ribbon
Paper Pizazz™ diagonal ribbons patterned paper
computer and printer
low temperature glue gun and sticks

Use the computer and printer to write a special "thank you" to your guests. Cut the paper to fit in the frame. Tie the ribbon in a shoestring bow (see inside the front cover). Glue it to the upper left corner of the frame.

Silver Place Card Frame

3 1/4"x3 1/4" silver heart frame with roses and pre-printed guest table card
7" of 1/4" wide lavender satin ribbon
fine point black pen
low temperature glue gun and sticks

Remove the card from the frame and use the black pen to complete. Replace the card in the frame and use the ribbon to make a shoestring bow (see inside the front cover). Glue it to the center of the heart top.

> **Designer Tip:** *Including a wedding photo in your thank you notes would allow your guests to use the frame as a remembrance of the occasion.*

Stamped Gift Bag

8"x10 1/2" blue-gray bag with handles
white tissue paper
2 yards of 6" wide silver tulle ribbon
2" wide double-heart foam stamp
metallic silver acrylic paint
paper plate
newspaper

1. Lay the bag flat on the newspaper. Pour a small amount of the paint onto the paper plate. Dip the heart stamp into the paint and stamp on the newspaper to blot the excess paint. Stamp randomly over the entire front of the bag, turning the stamp in different directions as you stamp. Let dry.

2. Cut the tulle ribbon in half and hold together as one. Wrap around the right front handle and tie a shoestring bow (see inside the front cover) with 4" loops and 6" tails. Cut the ends into inverted "V".

Stamped Gift Wrap

matte-finish white gift wrap
2" wide double-heart foam stamp
lavender acrylic paint
24" square of lavender tulle
16" of 1 1/2" of lavender satin ribbon
paper plate, newspapers

1. Cut the gift wrap to the appropriate size for the gift box. Place the wrap face up on the newspaper. Pour a small amount of paint onto the paper plate. Dip the stamp into paint and then stamp on the newspaper to blot the excess. Stamp the hearts randomly onto the gift wrap, turning the stamp in different directions as you stamp. Let dry.

2. Wrap the gift in the wrapping paper. Cut the tulle wide enough to be gathered up around the gift. Use the ribbon to tie a shoestring bow (see inside the front cover) with 2" loops. Cut the tails into an inverted "V".

Stamped Luminary

5"x10" ivory paper bag
2" wide double-heart sponge stamp
X-acto® knife and 5" square cutting surface
silver acrylic paint
tea light candle
paper plate, newspapers

1. Lay the bag flat on the newspaper. Pour a small amount of the paint onto the paper plate. Dip the heart stamp in silver paint and stamp on the newspaper to blot the excess paint. Stamp randomly over the entire front of the bag, turning the stamp in different directions as you stamp. Let dry.

2. Trace the heart pattern onto the bag front. Insert the cutting surface inside the bag and use the knife to cut the heart out. Open the bag and place the candle inside.

Silver Organza Bag

8"x12" silver organza drawstring bag with metallic
    silver cord and tassels
metallic silver gift wrap
3" wide white organza rose
3" wide silk ivy leaf
low temperature glue gun and sticks

1. Wrap the gift in the silver paper, then place it in the organza bag. Draw the strings and tie the cord in a shoestring bow (see inside the front cover) with 3" loops and 6" and 8" tails.

2. Glue the leaf and the rose just below the bow center with the leaf behind the rose.

Custom Bottle Label

5"x12" white organza bottle bag with drawstring
bottle of champagne or sparkling cider
three 1³/₄" wide variegated silk ivy leaves
computer and printer
solid white paper
Paper Pizazz™ specialty gold paper
tacky glue
low temperature glue gun and sticks

1. *To make a customized label:* Soak the label on the purchased bottle in water to loosen the glue, then peel it off. Print the name of the bride and groom on white paper (or a coordinating patterned paper) and cut into a strip large enough to cover where the original label had been. Mat the white paper on gold, leaving a ¹/₄" border. Glue the new label to the bottle using the tacky glue. Let the glue dry.

2. Place the bottle in the organza bag and draw the strings. Tie it in a shoestring bow (see inside the front cover). Glue one ivy leaf below the bow center and one on each side of the center leaf.

Designer Tip: Give these lovely bottles to the bridal party at the rehearsal or to special friends and relatives who helped with the wedding.

Favors & Keepsakes

Favors add a charming and graceful touch to the occasion, and making your own will help with your budget. There are numerous styles for you to choose from when deciding what you'd like to include in your wedding. Favors are generally presented in one of three forms. **Edible** favors of candy or nuts are individually portioned and embellished for each guest. These are given during the reception. **Memento** or keepsake favors are small gifts given by the bride and groom to their guests in remembrance of the occasion. **Celebration** favors are given for guest participation in honoring the bride and groom as they are pronounced husband and wife or at their departure.

Tulle and lace circles can be found in craft stores and make the task of assembling favors easy since they're already cut. Simply gather the tulle around the contents and tie it with a ribbon; embellish the bow with a flower, bell or small ring accent, and voila!—your favor is ready! It can be given out in this form or tucked into a small basket, box or one of the many little containers available to match the theme of your wedding. Producing the favors in assembly-line fashion makes this task easy and relatively quick while relieving your budget.

Tulle-Wrapped Bubbles

$2^{1/4}$" tall bottle of bubbles
one 9" wide lavender tulle circle
9" of $1/4$" wide lavender satin ribbon
one $5/8$" wide satin ribbon rose
low temperature glue gun and sticks

Place the bubble bottle in the center of the tulle circle. Gather up the edges around the bottle and tie with the ribbon in a shoestring bow (see inside the front cover) with 1" loops and tails. Glue the rose to the center of the bow.

Bubbles with Bubble Band

$2^{1/4}$" tall bottle of bubbles
$1^{3/4}$" wide white satin pre-made "Bubble Band" with satin flower and pearl center

Place the band over the neck of the bubbles.

Designer Tip: *Bubbles can be blown as the newly married couple walk down the aisle or as they make their get away. Use caution when choosing to use bubbles as floors can become slippery. Check with the church or facility staff to be sure it's permissible to use bubbles inside the building.*

Lavender Place Card Holder

2½" square cluster of lavender paper roses in leaf covered box
Paper Pizazz™ purple satin paper (by the sheet)
18" of ¼" wide lavender satin ribbon
low temperature glue gun and sticks

Tie the ribbon around the box and make into a shoestring bow (see inside the front cover). Print each guest's name and table number on coordinating patterned paper. Trim to a 1½"x2" rectangle and insert it behind the bow, using a dot of glue to secure.

Designer Tip: Using the computer makes it simple to unify the written information for your wedding. Select a font and use it for your invitations, programs, place cards and thank-yous.

White Favor

2½" square cluster of white paper roses in leaf covered box
16" of ⅛" wide white satin ribbon
½" wide pink paper rose with a 1" long leaf and wire stem
⅛" wide dowel or knitting needle
low temperature glue gun and sticks

Wrap the ribbon around the box and tie into a shoestring bow (see inside the front cover). Trim the rose stem to 2" long and wrap around the dowel to coil. Remove the dowel and pull the coil to loosen slightly, then glue the rose to the bow center.

Designer Tip: These are darling favors to give at bridal showers, rehearsal dinners or the wedding reception as a special keepsake.

Mauve Personalized Favor

2½" square cluster of mauve paper roses in leaf covered box
16" of ⅜" wide white picot satin ribbon
white paper
⅛" wide hole punch

Use the computer to type the bride and groom's names and wedding date. Print out on white paper. Cut it into 2¼"x1" rectangles and punch a hole at one end. Wrap the ribbon around the box, threading the tag onto the ribbon with the printing facing out. Tie the ribbon into a shoestring bow (see inside the front cover) with 1½" loops and tails.

Hand-Wrapped Bouquet

nine ⅝" wide paper roses, each with a 1" long leaf and 4" long wire stems: lavender, yellow, white and pink
9" of ¼" wide pink satin ribbon
green floral tape
pencil
wire cutters

Hold all of the flower stems together and wrap with floral tape to secure. Wrap the stem around the pencil to coil then remove the pencil and slightly pull apart the coil. Use the ribbon to tie into a shoestring bow (see inside the front cover) at the base of the bouquet.

> Designer Tip: *Use flowers that match the color scheme of your wedding for the perfect color-coordinated favor.*

Quick-to-Finish Bouquet

one rose and daisy floral pick with eight ⅝" wide yellow roses with 1" long leaves, many ¼" white daisies and a 4" long wrapped stem
12" of ⅛" wide white satin ribbon
⅛" wide hole punch
white paper
computer and printer
pencil

Wrap the bouquet stem around the pencil to coil. Slightly pull the coil apart. Print a thank you message on white or coordinating patterned paper. Cut into a 2"x1¼" rectangle and punch a hole at one end. Trim the corners on the hole-punched end as shown. Thread the tag onto the ribbon. Tie the ribbon at the base of the bouquet in a shoestring bow (see inside the front cover) with 1" loops and 4½" tails.

> Designer Tip: *Using pre-made bouquets makes assembling the favors quick and easy.*

Silver Trays & Silver Baskets

Basket with Flowers:
2 1/2"x2 1/8" silver heart-shaped basket with 1 3/4" tall handle
two 6" lengths of 1/4" wide pink satin ribbon
two 9" wide tulle circles
three 3/4" wide pink silk flowers
18 almonds
low temperature glue gun and sticks

Layer the tulle circles together and place the almonds in the center. Gather the edges up around the almonds, then tie the tulle with the ribbons in an overhand knot (see inside the front cover). Glue a flower at the knot center and place the bundle into the basket. Glue a flower at the base of each handle.

Tray with Swan & Mints:
3" wide round silver metal tray
one 1 3/4" tall clear acrylic swan
one 12" square of white tulle
9" of 1/4" wide white picot satin ribbon
one 1/2" wide yellow paper rose with a 1" long leaf
7 yellow mints
low temperature glue gun and sticks

Glue the swan to the center of the tray. Place the mints around the swan and the tray in the center of the tulle square. Wrap the tulle around the tray and tie with the ribbon in a shoestring bow (see inside the front cover). Glue the rose and leaf to the bow center, then trim the gathered tulle straight across 1" above the bow.

Tray with Chocolates:
3" wide round silver metal tray
one 1 1/2" wide white paper candy cup (will measure 2 1/2" wide when flattened)
12" wide white tulle square
9" of 1/4" wide white satin ribbon
3/4" wide burgundy felt rosebud with green leaves
3 chocolates
low temperature glue gun and sticks

Flatten the candy cup, place it on the tray and arrange the chocolates on the paper. Place the tray in the center of the tulle and gather up the sides around the tray. Tie the tulle with the ribbon in a shoestring bow (see inside the front cover). Glue the rose to the center of the bow.

Designer Tip: These very elegant favors are quick to make and will be a nice keepsake for your guests.

Basket with Wrapped Handle & Bows:
2 1/2"x2 1/8" silver heart-shaped basket with 1 3/4" tall handle
one 9" wide white tulle circle with metallic glitter flecks
36" of 1/8" wide ivory satin ribbon
18" of 1/8" wide white satin ribbon
12 almonds
low temperature glue gun and sticks

1. Starting at the base of one handle, glue one end of the ivory ribbon, then wrap it around the handle gluing at the opposite handle base. Cut two 9" lengths of both the ivory and white ribbons. Holding the ivory and white ribbon together as one, make a shoestring bow (see inside the front cover) and glue it to a handle base. Repeat using the remaining 9" ribbons on the opposite handle base.

2. Place the almonds in the center of the tulle. Gather the tulle edges around the almonds and tie with the remaining ivory ribbon in an overhand knot. Place the bundle in the basket.

Bells

Bells are a lovely way to send the bride and groom off on their honeymoon. If your reception venue will not allow birdseed or petals, try this musical send off.

White Bell with Crystal Berries and Tag:
$1^{1}/_{2}$" tall white bell with pre-printed tag
1" wide cluster with nine $^{1}/_{4}$" long clear berries, a green leaf and 1" long wire stem
9" of $^{3}/_{8}$" wide white picot satin ribbon
low temperature glue gun and sticks

Remove the cord and tag from the bell. Discard the cord. Using the ribbon, make a shoestring bow (see inside the front cover). Glue the bow to the top of the bell. Bend the berry stem into a curl and glue over the bow center. Glue the tag to extend from under the berry cluster as shown.

White Bell with Candy Wrapped in Tulle:
$1^{1}/_{4}$" tall white bell
one 9" wide white tulle circle
9" of $^{1}/_{4}$" wide white sheer ribbon
6-8 mints

Place the mints inside the bell. Place the bell on the center of the tulle circle. Gather the tulle edges up around bell and tie with the ribbon into a shoestring bow (see inside the front cover).

Gold Bell with Flower:
$1^{1}/_{4}$" tall gold bell with gold cord and pre-printed tag
two 9" lengths of $^{1}/_{4}$" wide white sheer ribbon
$^{3}/_{4}$" wide burgundy flower with yellow center and 1" long leaf
low temperature glue gun and sticks

Hold the ribbon lengths together and tie into a shoestring bow (see inside the front cover). Glue it to the top of the bell. Glue the flower to the bow center.

> **Designer Tip:** These favors fill two roles as both a candy treat and celebration favor.

Wrapped Chocolate with Bell:
$1^{1}/_{4}$" tall gold bell
one 9" wide white tulle circle with metallic glitter flecks
one wrapped chocolate in gold paper and brown wrapper
12" of $^{3}/_{8}$" wide white picot satin ribbon

Place the chocolate in the center of the tulle circle. Gather the tulle edges up around candy. Thread the bell onto the ribbon and wrap the ribbon around the tulle to secure and tie into a shoestring bow (see inside the front cover) with 1" loops and $1^{1}/_{2}$" tails.

Satin Organza Boxes

These pre-made boxes can be purchased (4 to a package) in colors to coordinate with your wedding. Here are a few ideas for filling them:

Periwinkle with Petals:
2 1/4"x1 5/8" periwinkle satin covered box with tulle lining and organza bow
handful of pink & ivory satin and organza rose petals (purchase by the box)

Untie the bow and fill the box with rose petals. Retie the bow.

> **Designer Tip:** The petals can be tossed at the bride and groom as they exit the church or the reception and the box makes a nice keepsake for the guests.

Yellow with Clay Rose:
2 1/4"x1 5/8" yellow satin covered box with tulle lining and organza bow
1/2 cup of small mints
3/4" wide yellow clay rose with 1" long leaf
low temperature glue gun and sticks

Untie the bow and fill the box with candy. Retie the bow. Glue the rose to the center of the bow.

White with Doves:
2 1/4"x1 5/8" white satin covered box with tulle lining and organza bow
1/2 cup of seasoned almonds
two gold plastic wedding rings with doves
low temperature glue guns and sticks

Untie the bow and fill the box with nuts. Retie the bow. Intertwine the rings by placing one dove inside the other ring. Point the doves in the same direction. Glue the rings together to secure. Glue them to the center of the bow.

Pink with Wedding "Kit":
2 1/4"x1 5/8" pink satin covered box with tulle lining and organza bow
personalized match book
one 2 1/4" tall bottle of bubbles
12 small mints
two 9" lengths of 1/4" wide pink satin ribbon
one 9" wide pink tulle circle

Tie one length of ribbon around the neck of the bubbles bottle and make into a shoestring bow (see inside the front cover). Place the candy in the center of the tulle circle and tie with the remaining ribbon, making a shoestring bow. Untie the box bow. Place the candy bundle, bubbles and matches in the satin box. Retie the bow.

Organza Bags

Large Bag with Petals:
5"x10" white organza bag with white satin ribbon drawstring
one $^7/_8$" wide mauve foam rose blossom with 1" long leaf
2 cups of pink & ivory silk and organza rose petals (purchased by the box)

Fill the bag with the petals and draw the strings, then tie in a shoestring bow (see inside the front cover). Glue the rose to the bow center.

> **Designer Tip:** *This celebratory favor can be given to the guests as they enter the church and the petals can be tossed as the couple makes their recession down the aisle. A beautiful tribute!*

Lavender Bag:
$3^1/_4$"x$3^1/_4$" lavender organza bag with lavender satin ribbon drawstring
one $^3/_4$" wide lavender silk flower and two 1" long leaves
Jordan almonds
low temperature glue gun and sticks

Fill the bag with the candy and draw the strings, then tie into a shoestring bow (see inside the front cover). Glue the flower to the bow center.

Pink Bag:
$3^1/_4$"x$3^1/_4$" pink organza bag with pink satin ribbon drawstring
three 8mm ivory flat-backed pearls
one 10mm ivory flat-backed pearl
2 tablespoons dried rose petals
low temperature glue gun and sticks

Glue the 8mm half pearls to the bottom edge of the bag. Fill the bag with the petals and draw the strings, then tie into a shoestring bow (see inside the front cover). Glue the 10mm pearl half to bow center.

Ivory Bag:
$3^1/_4$"x$3^1/_4$" ivory organza bag with ivory satin ribbon drawstring
green mints
one $^5/_8$" wide ivy leaf
low temperature glue gun and sticks

Fill the bag with the mints and draw the strings, then tie into a shoestring bow (see inside the front cover). Glue the ivy leaf to the bow center.

> *To dry rose petals: Pull unblemished petals from fresh roses and lay flat on a paper towel or newspapers. Allow to dry undisturbed for one week in a dry area.*

White Basket with Pink Flower

3"x1³/₄" white plastic basket with a 1¹/₄" tall handle
fifteen ³/₄" wide pink silk flowers
two 9" wide pink tulle circles
9" of ¹/₄" wide pink satin ribbon
4 Jordan almonds
low temperature glue gun and sticks

Glue the flowers around the rim of the basket. Layer the tulle circles together and place the candy in the center. Gather up the tulle edges and tie with the ribbon into a shoestring bow (see inside the front cover). Place the bundle in the basket.

Cinderella's Carriage

4¹/₂"x2¹/₂" clear acrylic horse drawn coach with hinged roof
³/₄" wide silk flowers with 1" long leaves: 2 white and 3 blue
18" of ¹/₄" wide white satin ribbon
white and blue Jordan almonds
26-gauge wire
low temperature glue gun and sticks

Use the ribbon to make a loopy bow (see inside the front cover) with six 1¹/₄" loops. Glue it to the roof of the carriage. Glue two blue and one white flower and two leaves to the bow center. Glue the remaining flowers between the horses, then fill the carriage with the Jordan almonds.

Basket with Lavender Bouquet

3"x1³/₄" white plastic basket with a 1¹/₄" tall handle
three ⁵/₈" wide lavender paper roses with three 1" long leaves and 3" long wire stems
two 9" wide lavender tulle circles
12" of ¹/₈" wide lavender satin ribbon
candy
¹/₈" wide dowel or knitting needle
green floral tape
low temperature glue gun and sticks

Hold the flower stems together as one and wrap with floral tape. Wrap the taped stems around the dowel in a spiral. Slightly pull the spirals apart. Use the ribbon to tie the bouquet to the base of the basket handle in a shoestring bow (see inside the front cover). Layer the tulle circles together and place the candy in the center. Gather up the edges and tie with the remaining ribbon in an overhand knot.

Box Favors

These make lovely favor boxes for candy or gift boxes for attendant's gifts.

Iridescent Box with Rose:
3¼"x5½" iridescent white box with handles
¾" wide pink foam rose blossom with 1" long leaf
two 9" wide pink tulle circles
18" of ⅛" wide white satin ribbon
candy or gift
26-gauge wire
low temperature glue gun and sticks

Use the ribbon to make a loopy bow (see inside the front cover) with six 1½" long loops. Glue it to the box front 1¼" from the top edge. Glue the rose to the bow center. Wrap the candy or small gift in the tulle circles and place in the box.

Clear box with Peppermints:
2" wide clear acrylic box with sheer white bow on top
8 red & white peppermint candies

Fill this pre-made box with peppermint candies or your favorite candy.

Heart Box with Roses & Ivy:
3¼"x5½" white box with silver hearts and handles
two 9" wide white tulle circles with metallic glitter flecks
one 2" wide variegated ivy leaf
one 1¼" wide English ivy leaf
½" wide burgundy rosebud with three ¾" long leaves
candy or gift
low temperature glue gun or sticks

Glue the variegated ivy leaf to the upper left corner of the box front. Glue the English ivy leaf over the first. Glue the rosebud and leaves to the base of the leaves. Layer the tulle circles and place the candy or gift in the center, then place in the box.

Swans & Slippers

Swan with flowers at neck:
$3^{3}/_{4}$" wide clear acrylic swan favor cup
five $^{3}/_{4}$" wide white silk flowers
9" of $^{3}/_{8}$" wide white picot satin ribbon
one 9" wide white tulle circle
five Jordan almonds
low temp glue gun and sticks

Glue four flower blossoms around the base of the swan's neck. Place the candy in the center of the tulle circle. Gather up the edges and, using the ribbon, tie a shoestring bow (see inside the front cover). Place the bundle in the swan cup.

Swan with Bouquet of Flowers:
$3^{3}/_{4}$" wide clear acrylic swan favor cup
one rose and daisy floral pick with eight $^{5}/_{8}$" wide yellow roses with 1" long leaves, many $^{1}/_{4}$" white daisies and a 4" long wrapped stem
9" of $^{1}/_{4}$" wide white silk ribbon
low temperature glue gun and sticks

Trim one daisy off of the bouquet and set aside. Cut the bouquet stem to $^{1}/_{2}$" long and glue the flowers into the swan cup. Using the ribbon, tie a shoestring bow (see inside the front cover) around the swan's neck. Glue the single daisy to the center of the bow.

Glass Slipper with Pink Flower:
$3^{1}/_{4}$" long clear acrylic slipper
one 9" wide pink tulle circle
6" of $^{1}/_{4}$" wide pink satin ribbon
one $^{3}/_{4}$" wide pink silk flower with yellow center
four Jordan almonds
low temperature glue gun and sticks

Place the almonds in the center of the tulle and gather up the edges around the candy. Tie the ribbon into an overhand knot (see inside the front cover) as shown. Glue the flower to the toe. Place the bundle in the slipper.

Tulle Wrapped Glass Slipper:
$3^{1}/_{4}$" long clear acrylic slipper
12" white tulle square
9" of $^{1}/_{4}$" wide white sheer ribbon
four Jordan almonds

Place the almonds lined up in the slipper. Place the slipper on the center of the tulle and gather the edges up around the sides. Tie the ribbon into a shoestring bow (see inside the front cover) as shown.

Champagne Glasses

Champagne Glass with Blue Tulle:
2" tall clear acrylic champagne glass
two 9" wide light blue tulle circles
9" of 1/4" wide white satin ribbon
Jordan almonds: 2 white, 2 light blue
scissors

Layer the tulle circles together. Use the scissors to make a 1" slit in the center through both layers of tulle. Thread the glass bottom and stem through the slit and gather the edges up around the bowl. Fill the glass with the candy. Tie the ribbon into a shoestring bow (see inside the front cover) around the tulle as shown.

Champagne Glass with Peppermints:
2" tall clear acrylic champagne glass
one 9" wide white tulle circle
6" of 7/8" wide forest green satin ribbon
three red & white peppermint candies
scissors

Cut a 1" wide slit in the center of the tulle circle. Thread the glass bottom and stem through the slit. Fill the glass with candy and gather the edges up around the bowl. Tie the ribbon into an overhand knot (see inside the front cover) around the tulle as shown. Trim the tails into an inverted "V".

Designer Tip: **This is a very quick and easy holiday wedding favor to make. Consider using green mints and your wedding color ribbon for a custom look.**

Champagne Glass with Swan:
2" tall clear acrylic champagne glass
1 1/2" tall ivory acrylic swan
seven 3/4" wide white silk flowers
one 9" wide white lace circle
one 9" wide white tulle circle
9" of 1/4" wide white satin ribbon
4 white Jordan almonds
low temperature glue gun and sticks

Layer the tulle circle on the lace circle, then place the candy in the center. Turn the glass upside-down and place it over the candy. Gather the circles up around the stem above the bowl of the glass. Tie the ribbon into a shoestring bow (see inside the front cover). Glue the swan to the top of the glass base. Glue the flowers around the base of the swan as shown.

Wrapped Champagne Glass with Chocolate:
2" tall clear acrylic champagne glass
one 9" wide white tulle circle with metallic glitter flecks
9" of 1/4" wide white satin ribbon
one chocolate bon bon

Place the bon bon in the glass and cover with the tulle circle. Wrap the circle down around the glass and, using the ribbon, tie a shoestring bow (see inside the front cover) with 1" loops and tails around the stem as shown.

Votive Cup with Candy

2"x2½" clear glass votive cup
one 12" square of white tulle
12" of ¼" wide pink satin ribbon
one ¾" wide pink foam rose with one 1" long leaf
pink mints
low temperature glue gun and sticks

Place the mints in the votive cup. Place the cup on the center of the tulle. Gather the edges up around the cup and tie with the ribbon into a shoestring bow (see inside the front cover) with 2" loops and tails. Glue the rose and leaf to the bow center.

Birdseed Bundle with Dove

one 9" wide white tulle circle
9" of ¼" wide white satin ribbon
one gold plastic wedding ring with dove
2 tablespoons of birdseed
low temperature glue gun and sticks

Place the birdseed in the center of the tulle. Gather up the edges and tie with the ribbon into a shoestring bow (seee inside the front cover). Glue the ring with the dove to the bow center.

Candle with Cherub

1½" tall mauve votive candle
two 9" wide white tulle circles
9" of ¼" wide pink satin ribbon
one 1" long white plastic cherub
low temperature glue gun and sticks

Layer the tulle circles together. Place the candle in the center of the circles. Gather up the tulle and tie with the ribbon into a shoestring bow (see inside the front cover). Glue the top of the cherub under the bow as shown.

> **Designer Tip:** *Chose candle scents to suit the season of your wedding—floral fragrances for spring and summer; spicy for fall and winter.*

Blue Bundle with Doves

two 9" wide blue tulle circles
9" of 1/4" wide white satin ribbon
two 1" wide white plastic doves
5 Jordan almonds
low temperature glue gun and sticks

Layer the tulle circles together. Place the candy in center and gather the edges up around the candy. Tie with the ribbon in a shoestring bow (see inside the front cover). Fan out the tulle edges and glue the doves at the center of the gathered tulle as shown.

Candy with Lace & Cherub

one 9" wide white lace circle
one 9" wide white tulle circle
9" of 3/8" wide white picot satin ribbon
one 1" long white plastic cherub with a silver cord
5 yellow mints
low temperature glue gun and sticks

Layer the tulle circle over the lace circle. Place the candy in the center and gather both edges up around the candy. Tie with the ribbon into a shoestring bow (see inside the front cover). Shorten the cherub's cord to 1/2" long and glue the cord under the bow as shown.

Lace Roll

one 9" wide white lace circle
18" of 1/4" wide white satin ribbon
9 green Jordan almonds

Place the candy along the center of the lace circle in a line. Fold the circle in half and roll up. Cut the ribbon in half and tie each end into a shoestring bow (see inside the front cover).

Bundle in Champagne Glass

2" tall clear acrylic champagne glass
9" wide white lace circle
9" wide white tulle circle
3/4" wide white silk flower
9" of 1/8" wide white satin ribbon
one pre-printed "Thank You" tag
9 white mints
low temperature glue gun and sticks

Layer the tulle circle over the lace circle. Place the candy in the center and gather up the edges. Place the ribbon through the hole on the tag. Tie the bundle with the ribbon into a shoestring bow (see inside the front cover) with the printed side of the tag face out. Glue the flower to the center of the bow.

Pink Ribbon Streamer Bundle

three 9" wide pink tulle circles
18" of 1/4" wide pink satin ribbon
18" of 1/8" wide white satin ribbon
one 3/4" wide pink silk flower
one 1" wide ivy leaf
8 pink mints
low temperature glue gun and sticks

Layer the three tulle circles together. Place the candy in the center and gather the edges. Holding both lengths of ribbon together as one, tie a shoestring bow (see inside the front cover) with 1 1/2" loops and 6" long tails as shown. Knot the tail ends 1" from the end. Glue the ivy leaf and the flower to the bow center.

Lace Bundle with Streamers

one 9" wide white tulle circle
one 9" wide white lace circle
18" of 1/8" wide ivory satin ribbon
18" of 1/4" wide ivory sheer ribbon
one 3/4" wide ivory clay flower with two 1" long leaves
eight yellow mints
low temperature glue gun and sticks

Layer the tulle circle on the lace circle. Place the candy in the center and gather up the edges. Holding both lengths of ribbon together as one, tie into a shoestring bow (see inside the front cover) with 1 1/2" loops and 6" tails as shown. Knot each tail 3/4" from the end, then glue the leaves and the rose to the center of the bow.